ATTACK OF THE

VIRUSES

By
William Anthony

BookLife
PUBLISHING

©2022
BookLife Publishing Ltd.
King's Lynn
Norfolk, PE30 4LS

ISBN: 978-1-80155-127-4

Written by:
William Anthony

Edited by:
Madeline Tyler

Designed by:
Amy Li

A catalogue record for this book is available from the British Library.

All rights reserved. Printed in Poland.

All facts, statistics, web addresses and URLs in this book were verified as valid and accurate at time of writing. No responsibility for any changes to external websites or references can be accepted by either the author or publisher.

PHOTO CREDITS

All images courtesy of Shutterstock. With thanks to Getty Images, Thinkstock Photo and iStockphoto.

Used throughout (including cover) – chekart (background), Sonechko57 (slime), VectorShow (microbe characters), Alena Ohneva (vector microbes), Olga_C (circle image frame).
Used throughout (excluding cover) – Photo Melon (clipboard), Lorelyn Medina (scientist characters). P4–5 – Imagerist, Naeblys, p6–7 – ASDF_MEDIA, Peeradach R, p8–9 – svtdesign, antpkr, ranjith ravindran, p10–11 – pornpan chaiu-dom, MaryValery, p12–13 – Marcel Jancovic, Dermatology11, Real Illusion, p14–15 – What's My Name, nobeastoffierce, VectorShow, p16–17 – Arit FongFung, MTPhoto_Life, p18–19 – MaryAnne Campbell, Svineyard, p20–21 – pinkeyes, wavebreakmedia, p22–23 – didesigns021, Africa Studio.

CONTENTS

MINI MONSTERS

Look around you. What is the smallest thing you can see? Did you know there are thousands of smaller things you cannot see? Some of them are microorganisms. Micro means tiny, and organism means a living thing.

Microorganisms are sometimes called microbes, and they are everywhere. They are on the floor, our desks and our clothes. They even live on our skin and in our bodies.

VULGAR
VIRUSES

Viruses are a type of microorganism. Like other microorganisms, they are too small to see. Viruses can cause bad things to happen if they get inside our bodies.

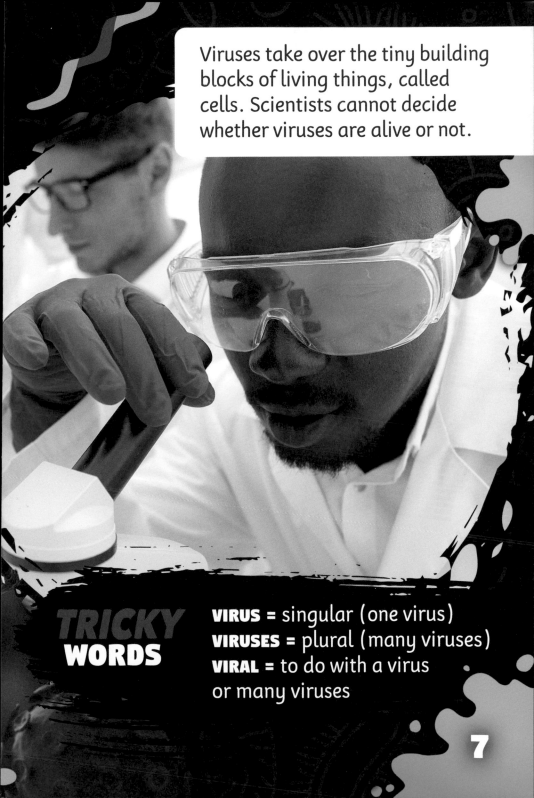

Viruses take over the tiny building blocks of living things, called cells. Scientists cannot decide whether viruses are alive or not.

TRICKY WORDS

VIRUS = singular (one virus)
VIRUSES = plural (many viruses)
VIRAL = to do with a virus or many viruses

Viruses can spread in lots of different ways. They can be spread by coughing, sneezing, touching other people, or touching things without washing your hands afterwards.

We cannot treat viral infections in the same way that we treat other infections. Antibiotics are a type of medicine we can use for bacterial infections, but they do not work on viruses.

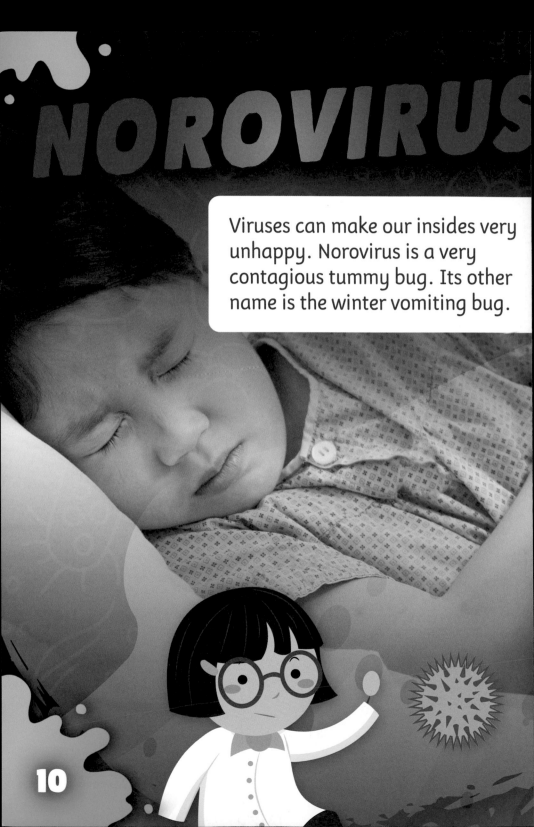

NOROVIRUS

Viruses can make our insides very unhappy. Norovirus is a very contagious tummy bug. Its other name is the winter vomiting bug.

The effects of norovirus are not pretty. They include vomiting, more vomiting, diarrhoea (runny poo) and a lot more vomiting.

WARTS AND VERRUCAS

Viruses do not just affect the inside of our bodies – they can affect the outside too. Warts and verrucas are caused by a virus and are spread by touching.

WART

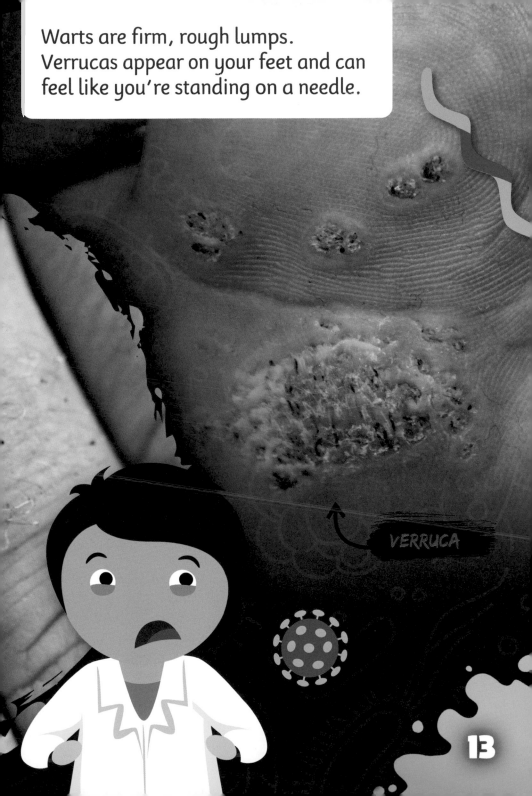

RABIES

Viruses can invade animals and make them very ill. Rabies is a dangerous virus that can be spread by the spit of infected animals.

RABIES

Dogs can get rabies if they are bitten by another animal that has it. Rabies can cause unusual anger, a high temperature, difficulty swallowing and difficulty moving.

CHICKENPOX

Have you or any of your friends ever had a rash with lots of spots? It could be chickenpox. It is completely normal in children. Chickenpox usually goes away after two weeks, and most people never get it again.

Chickenpox might start like a normal cold, with lots of sneezing and coughing. After a few days, a rash starts. It is important not to scratch the spots.

ROSE ROSETTE

Viruses can attack almost any living thing, including plants. Rose rosette is a viral disease in rose plants.

The disease is spread by mites. It causes parts of the plant to crinkle up and grow the wrong way. Most of the time, the virus kills the rose.

19

FLU

One of the most common viral illnesses is flu. It is spread by the coughs and sneezes of people who have flu.

Flu can be very unpleasant. It can cause a high temperature, a headache, coughing, sneezing, a sore throat, aches and tiredness. There is a vaccine that people can have to protect them from getting very ill with flu.

STRIKING BACK

Viruses are not easy to treat, so we try to stop ourselves getting infected in the first place. Vaccines can help keep us safe from viruses.

When we do get infected, there are some treatments we can use to help us with any symptoms. The fight against viruses has begun!

QUESTIONS

1: Where do verrucas appear?

2: Which of these can be a sign of rabies:
   a) Turning green
   b) Unusual anger
   c) Hands falling off

3: Can you name a virus that gives you red, itchy spots?

4: Can you name three ways that a virus can spread?

5: Have you ever had a virus? What did it feel like?

BookLife
freedom
Readers